12 STORIES ABOUT HELPING IN EDUCATION

by Patricia Hutchison

12 STORY LIBRARY
MORE TO EXPLORE

www.12StoryLibrary.com

12-Story Library is an imprint of Bookstaves.

Photographs ©: Denis Farrell/Associated Press, cover, 1; Senior Corps/PD, 4; Corporation for National and Community Service/YouTube, 4; Corporation for National and Community Service/YouTube, 5; WCCO - CBS Minnesota/YouTube, 6; Brainsil/Shutterstock.com, 7; WCCO - CBS Minnesota/YouTube, 7; Barbara Bush Foundation for Family Literacy/YouTube, 8; The US National Archives/PD, 8; GivingLibrary/YouTube, 9; WXII 12 News/YouTube, 10; Katharine Tamez/Shutterstock.com, 10; Bill Zandi/YouTube, 11; Denis Farrell/Associated Press, 12; Ossewa/CC3.0, 12; OWN/YouTube, 13; NDPC/YouTube, 14; Monkey Business Images/Shutterstock.com, 14; Monkey Business Images/Shutterstock.com, 15; GivingLibrary/YouTube, 16; First5CoCo/YouTube, 17; PD, 18; The Real News Network/YouTube, 18; Jeff Lange/Akron Beacon Journal/Associated Press, 19; arun sambhu mishra/Shutterstock.com, 20; CRS PHOTO/Shutterstock.com, 21; WBFO/YouTube, 22; RADIO.COM/YouTube, 22; RADIO.COM/YouTube, 23; PositiveTomorrows/YouTube, 24; Stand Together Foundation/YouTube, 24; PositiveTomorrows/YouTube, 25; JAZZ HOUSE KiDS/YouTube, 26; Steve Adubato/YouTube, 26; Montclair Film/CC2.0, 27; Monkey Business Images/Shutterstock.com, 28; LightField Studios/Shutterstock.com, 29

ISBN
9781632357458 (hardcover)
9781632358547 (paperback)
9781645820307 (ebook)

Library of Congress Control Number: 2019938679

Printed in the United States of America
October 2019

About the Cover

Oprah Winfrey cuts the ribbon at the grand opening of her Leadership Academy for Girls in South Africa.

Access free, up-to-date content on this topic plus a full digital version of this book. Scan the QR code on page 31 or use your school's login at 12StoryLibrary.com.

Table of Contents

1

Foster Grandparents Program: Everyone Wins

Senior citizens, wearing blue aprons and big smiles, greet children as they enter school. The children hug them. They call them Grandma and Grandpa. Some whisper secrets in their ears. The seniors are part of the Foster Grandparents Program. The program is part of Senior Corps, a US government agency. Its mission is to help senior citizens and promote a sense of community.

Most foster grandparents are assigned to schools or day-care centers. They are mentors to needy children. The grandparents read to them and help them write their names. Over time, children improve their language and social skills. They get higher scores on standardized

tests. This guides them toward success in high school and beyond.

The Foster Grandparents are paid a small amount. Many need the extra spending money. They also receive an annual physical, which keeps them healthy. If they can't afford the exam, the program pays for it.

The seniors like being more involved in their communities. Many enjoy a more active lifestyle. They say the program makes them feel respected and useful.

LEARNING HOW TO HELP

Before they start work in a classroom, Foster Grandparents must attend a training session. It prepares them to work well with children. They learn to spot signs that a child may be upset. This helps them to develop good relationships with the students.

20,000+
Number of seniors who volunteer as Foster Grandparents

- The seniors range in age from 55 to 93.
- Most spend 15 to 30 hours a week in the schools.
- The program is funded by the US government. There are Foster Grandparents in almost every state.

2 The Page Education Foundation: Helping Students of Color

Alan Page was a Minnesota Supreme Court Justice for 22 years. He was the state's first black supreme court justice. Before then, he was a professional football player. A member of the NFL Hall of Fame, Page has enough awards to fill an entire wall. But he is most proud of the work he does with students. In 1988, Page and his wife, Diane Sims, founded the Page Education Foundation. The organization helps students of color go to college.

The foundation awards annual, renewable grants up to $2,500. Students who receive the grants are called Page Scholars. They must perform 50 hours of community service each year. Page Scholars volunteer as tutors and mentors to younger children. They work with the children on reading, writing, and critical thinking. Having positive role models helps the children learn how to make good decisions and avoid

Alan Page takes a selfie with a group of Page Scholars.

$15 million+

Amount of scholarship money given to Page Scholars since 1988

- More than 7,000 students have been named Page Scholars.
- The scholars have spent over 470,000 hours volunteering.
- They work in community organizations and schools across Minnesota.

SHARING HIS AWARD

In 2018, Justice Alan Page received the Presidential Medal of Freedom. It is one of the highest awards that can be given to a civilian. At an assembly, Page presented the award to the students at Justice Page Middle School.

bad ones. Over 1,000 students apply every year to be Page Scholars. About half of them receive awards.

In 2017, a school in Minneapolis was renamed Justice Page Middle School. Students there are expected to set and achieve positive goals. Another important part of the program is learning how to form healthy relationships with others. Justice Page visits the school as often as he can. The students see him as a role model.

3 Barbara Bush: First Lady for Literacy

AaBbCc

BARBARA BUSH FOUNDATION FOR FAMILY LITERACY

LIFE. LIBERTY. **LITERACY.**

Barbara Bush knew the United States would be better off if everyone knew how to read and write. She felt illiteracy was the root of almost every problem. She believed many people committed crimes because they didn't have jobs. They didn't have jobs because they couldn't read and write. If the United States was going to compete in the world, its citizens must be educated.

Bush became First Lady in 1989, when her husband, George H. W. Bush, was elected president. She started a campaign to reduce illiteracy. She appeared on national TV. She performed on a national

radio program. On the radio, Bush was joined by Winnie-the-Pooh and other stars. She read stories aloud and discussed them with her guests. She gave parents tips for reading with their children.

The First Lady started the Barbara Bush Foundation for Family Literacy. The organization raises money from businesses. The money supports literacy programs. It pays for low-income parents and their children to attend school together. Both the children and the adults improve their reading abilities.

Another foundation program is called Teen Trendsetters. Elementary students are paired with teenage mentors. Most of the younger students improve their reading by one grade level. The teen mentors have high graduation rates. Bush chaired the foundation until 2012. Even after that, she remained active, working to improve literacy.

23

Millions of Americans in 1989 who could not read past fourth-grade level

- Millions more could not read above eighth-grade level.
- At that time, 30 percent of students dropped out of high school.
- Barbara Bush formed literacy programs in 48 states, Guam, and the District of Columbia.

THINK ABOUT IT

Barbara Bush blamed illiteracy for many problems in the United States. What other problems do countries face today? What can be done to help with these problems?

4

Students Helping Students: Aid for Schools in Need

Bill Zandi in 2012.

Bill Zandi was a high school freshman in 2005. That year, Hurricane Katrina damaged 110 of the 126 public schools in New Orleans. Wanting to help, Zandi called the Louisiana Department of Education. They told him the schools needed supplies. At the time, Zandi's high school was getting rid of materials they no longer needed. He asked his principal if he could send them to New Orleans. By June 2006, Zandi had raised $30,000. He sent two tractor trailers full of materials to New Orleans.

Zandi wanted to continue his work. He formed Students Helping Students (SHS). Zandi saw schools in poorer neighborhoods that didn't have basic supplies. They lacked things such as maps and reference books. SHS began to focus on more than just disaster relief.

SHS pairs clubs in wealthy schools with those at low-income schools. Clubs in the wealthier schools collect gently used supplies and furniture. Then they deliver them to the clubs they are paired with. SHS also runs a program called the School Funding Initiative. It gives grants to teachers at poorer schools for classroom supplies. The grant money comes from businesses. Each business agrees to sponsor a school assigned by SHS. The school receives $10,000 over the calendar year to help with basic needs.

SHS also has a mentoring program. Students in low-income schools get help with their homework. Mentors experience life outside their wealthy neighborhoods. It helps them understand that poverty exists not far from their homes.

$25,000

Value of books donated by SHS to schools in Louisiana by 2009

- Students Helping Students hosts bookfairs where textbooks and library books are provided to low-income schools.
- Nearly 4,000 books are distributed at each bookfair.
- SHS has also sent supplies to schools in North Carolina, Florida, and Pennsylvania.

5 Oprah Winfrey Leadership Academy: Helping Girls Succeed

Oprah Winfrey opens her Leadership Academy for Girls.

During her lifetime, Oprah Winfrey has donated millions of dollars to many causes. But she has said the bonds she forms with the girls in her academy are her greatest joy.

The media giant opened the Oprah Winfrey Leadership Academy for Girls (OWLAG) in 2007. Located just outside Johannesburg, South Africa, the boarding school serves girls in grades 8 to 12. All come from poor communities. Many grew up in thatch-roofed huts. Some have been abused. Others have lost their parents. Winfrey sees something special in all of them.

The campus of the Leadership Academy has 28 modern buildings. Every student takes part in music and sports programs. She must perform at least 10 hours of community service each term.

$140 million+
Amount Oprah Winfrey has contributed to OWLAG

- Winfrey was inspired to start the academy by Nelson Mandela.
- She pays for all the girls' clothing, uniforms, and medical bills.
- The Oprah Winfrey Leadership Academy Foundation (OWLAF) helps the girls through college.

THINK ABOUT IT

Nelson Mandela believed that education has the power to change the world. Do you agree? What is one way education can change the world?

Debates about global issues and ideas for how to promote greener living are parts of the curriculum.

Winfrey visits OWLAG when she can. She spends time chatting with the girls and teaching them life lessons. She shows them that their lives have value. Winfrey is like a mother to the girls. Many of them call her "Mum O."

The academy has a 100 percent graduation rate. Many of the girls go on to attend major universities. They earn advanced degrees and get jobs in business and government. But to Winfrey, that's not the most important thing. She tells the girls to be the CEOs of their own lives. She wants them to be happy.

Winfrey with Nelson Mandela.

6

National Dropout Prevention Center: Keeping Kids in School

In the United States, 15 percent of students who start ninth grade never finish high school. Some drop out because they are so far behind they feel they will never catch up. Others don't see the value in getting a diploma. To address this issue, the National Dropout Prevention Center (NDPC) was formed in 1986. Based at Clemson University in South Carolina, it works to increase the graduation rate in America's schools. It is a resource for schools across the country.

NDPC's mentoring program helps keep students from dropping out of school. The program matches college students with at-risk youth aged 10 to 18. The pairs meet one night a week on the college campus. They eat dinner together and work

on homework. Mentoring has helped many at-risk students improve their attendance. The students feel better knowing that someone cares about how they are doing in school.

Some students don't learn well in a traditional school. Sometimes family problems prevent them from attending. Some need a different setting, time, or pace for learning. Alternative schools supported by the NDPC give these students a different path to graduation. The schools are smaller. Students can get to know their teachers. Classes are offered year-round, with flexible hours. Students with jobs or children can work around their schedules.

$8,000

How much more high school graduates earn each year than non-graduates, on average

- In 2016–17, Iowa had the highest high school graduation rate: 91 percent.
- New Mexico had the lowest high school graduation rate: 71 percent.
- The average across the United States was 85 percent.

IT'S COOL TO STAY IN SCHOOL

According to the NDPC, students who drop out tend to struggle as adults. They earn less money than workers with diplomas. Dropouts also tend to have health problems. They are more likely to become alcoholics and have problems related to smoking.

7

Family Literacy: Schooling Parents So Kids Can Learn

At an elementary school in Oakland, California, adult women practice spelling. They are the mothers and grandmothers of children in the school. The women are immigrants. They come from Mexico, the Middle East, and Asia. They drop their children off at their classes. Then they go to their own classrooms to learn English.

School districts across the United States offer family classes in literacy. The adult learners have different levels of English understanding. Some classes start with the basics, such as letters and sounds. They also teach parents how to use translation programs on computers or smartphones.

Once the parents are more comfortable with the language, they are given real-world assignments. Most have to do with their children's education. For example, a parent

Parents practice English by reading to their preschoolers.

might have to send the child's teacher an email in English. Another might be asked to prepare questions for a meeting with the principal.

The parents' learning helps families in many ways. The program has a positive impact on the children's success in school. Parents can understand when their children speak English. They can help more with homework. Children get higher grades and have better attendance. There are benefits for the parents, too. Many go on to receive a GED, which is like a high school diploma. Some even go to college or technical school. With more education, they can get better jobs.

100

Number of school districts that offer family literacy classes

- Parents in the classes report that they read with their children often.
- They also talk to their children about school at least once a week.
- Parents said they speak English in the community more than twice a month.

8

The I Promise School: LeBron James Gives Back

THE I PROMISE SCHOOL

At age 33, basketball superstar LeBron James felt the first-day-of-school butterflies. It was the fall of 2018, and the doors of his I Promise school were about to open. Although James's school was part of the Akron, Ohio, school system, it wasn't the usual public school. It was especially for some of the city's most challenged students. These students were reading one or two years below their grade level. They had behavior problems. Some were already believed to be at risk for not graduating. James wanted them to have a better chance.

James knows that kids can form bad habits when they are left alone. So the I Promise school day is long. It runs from 9 a.m. until 5 p.m. The school year lasts from July 30 to May 17. Students attend summer school for seven weeks. Every day is a celebration. The kids are greeted with music and hi-fives.

Parents also receive help at I Promise. One room is filled with jackets and pants. Bread and peanut

WHAT'S IN A NAME?

The school's name, I Promise, comes from the promises the students are encouraged to make. They pledge to go to school, do their homework, and listen to their teachers. They promise to ask questions, be respectful of others, and live a healthy life.

$600,000

Financial support I Promise receives from the LeBron James Family Foundation

- The money helps to reduce class sizes.
- It pays for an hour of after-school tutoring for each student.
- In the first year, most I Promise students improved their test scores.

butter line the shelves. Parents can go anytime and pick up what they need. GED classes are offered. There is even a barbershop on site. The LeBron James Family Foundation pays for all of this. It is James's way of giving back to his hometown.

James plays basketball with I Promise students in 2019.

9

Teaching Happiness: A New Kind of Class

Students in India meditate.

Most schools in India are strict and challenging. Universities only accept students with test scores of 98 percent or above. Many students have high levels of stress. But schools in Delhi are offering classes on how to be happy. Teachers read uplifting stories. Students meditate while picturing something that makes them happy. There are no textbooks, grades, or tests for these classes.

Another school in India is taking happiness one step farther. It will be a new kind of school. It will have a meditation room filled with trees, and a test kitchen. One thing it won't have is a traditional classroom.

The school is being built in a rural area outside the city of Chennai. It is scheduled to open in 2020. Its first purpose is to teach children how to be happy. The founders believe that happiness helps people to build great lives. They want their graduates to go out into the world and do good.

The school will have no standard curriculum. Students will decide

1,000

Number of schools in Delhi that teach happiness classes

- The classes are taught at the beginning of the school day.
- They last 30 to 45 minutes.
- The focus is on creativity and wellness instead of math and science.

HAPPINESS IS PART OF EVERY SCHOOL DAY

At a school in London, students meditate every day. Physical activities help relieve stress. Teachers encourage kids to perform random acts of kindness. Every Friday, students are asked to think about three things that have gone well for them. This helps train their brains to think more positively.

what they want to learn. An ordinary day might start with a game of basketball. After that, some students will launch rockets. Others will recite poetry or learn how to dance. Instructors will act more like coaches. They won't teach information. Instead, they will help students learn how to learn.

10 Getting Kids to Read: A Vending Machine with Books

There is a new kind of vending machine in schools throughout the United States. But it doesn't dispense sodas or sugary treats. Instead, it gives out books. A school in Buffalo, New York, was one of the first to try out the idea. Studies showed that nearly 30 percent of adults in the area could not read and write. Staff members tried to think of ways to get kids reading. They knew that families often didn't have money to buy books. So they came up with the idea of a book vending machine.

The school bought a machine and stocked it with books. Then they held a ribbon-cutting ceremony and opened it for business. Students are given special coins to put into the slot. They select their book, push a button, and out it comes. Students

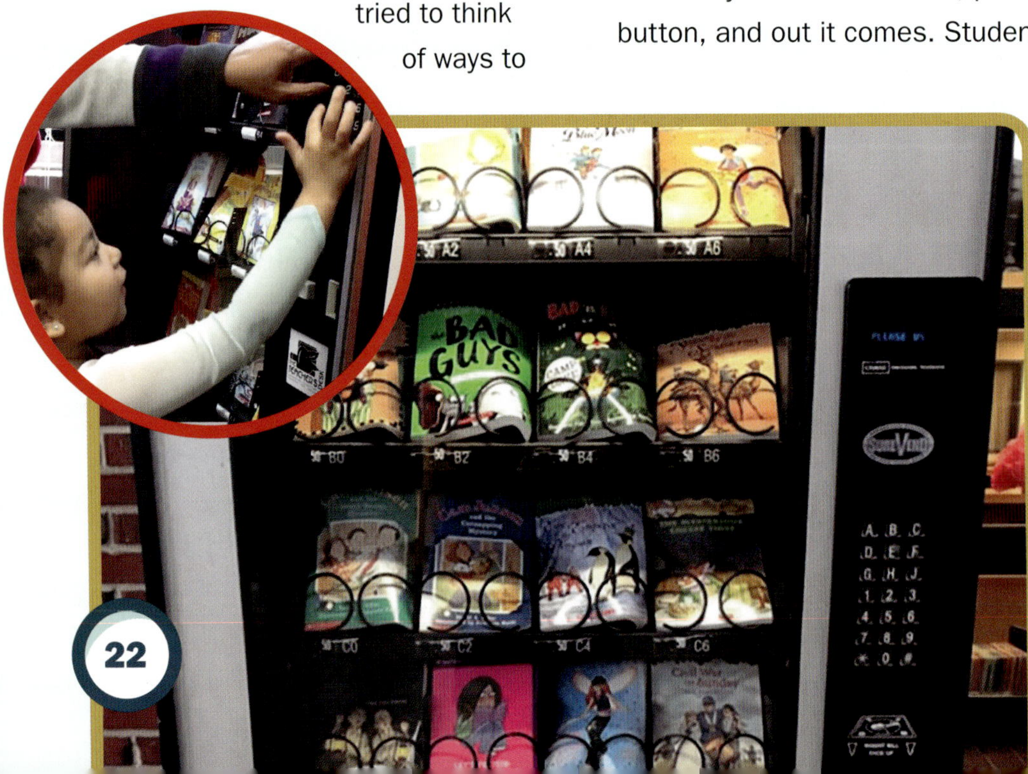

don't need to do anything special to receive a coin. Everyone gets a chance to get a free book. The students can take the books home and keep them. This encourages them to start their own libraries.

BOOKS FOR GOOD CHOICES

A school in Florida also has a book vending machine. Students are rewarded for making good choices. If they are kind to others, or get their homework done on time, they earn school money called "Bulldog Bucks." They give their bucks to the media specialist. Then they receive a coin to buy a book from the machine.

100

Number of books the machine in Buffalo "sold" on the first day

- The books are chosen by the school's media specialist.
- The specialist's choices are based on books borrowed most from the library.
- The machine dispenses both fiction and nonfiction books.

11

Positive Tomorrows: A School by and for Homeless Kids

Oklahoma City has a new school. It will serve nearly 200 kids experiencing homelessness. For many of them, school is not important. They are busy just trying to survive. An organization called Positive Tomorrows built the school. Programs focus on helping kids grow in positive ways. The organization also provides support

5,031

Number of homeless children enrolled in Oklahoma City's public schools in 2017

- Positive Tomorrows believes the number of homeless children in the city could be much higher. It could be closer to 10,000.
- The organization provides students with transportation to and from school.
- It hopes to expand its program to help even more homeless kids.

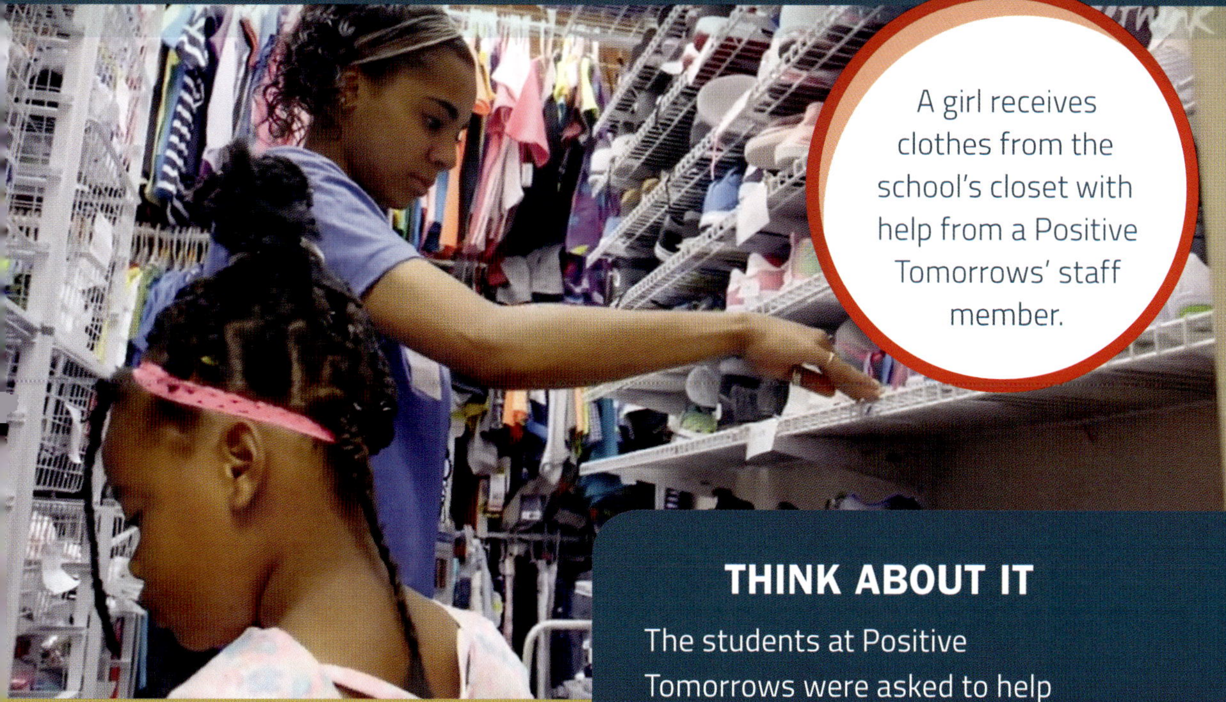

A girl receives clothes from the school's closet with help from a Positive Tomorrows' staff member.

services to families. These are not part of the regular public school programs.

THINK ABOUT IT

The students at Positive Tomorrows were asked to help design their new school. If you could design your school, what is one thing you would include? Give reasons for your choice.

Positive Tomorrows asked the students to help design the building. The kids made drawings that showed how they wanted their school to look. Many students wanted a treehouse, so one was built indoors. It serves as a place for kids to hang out and socialize. Another comfortable area is called the clubhouse. It has a small library. The kids can check out a book and keep it if they like.

Along with classrooms, the new school has fully furnished living rooms. These areas can be used by both students and their parents. They can cook, eat dinner, and spend time together. This is a rare event for families that are constantly moving from one shelter to the next.

Studies at the school focus on more than math and science. The students also work on life skills. They start by learning how to get up and get ready for school.

12

Jazz House Kids: Teaching Children about Jazz

In 1999, a New Jersey radio station asked Melissa Walker to create a new program. It would introduce kids to jazz. Walker was a jazz singer. She wanted to sing, not teach. But she finally gave in. As she worked with the children, she realized how little they knew about music, especially jazz. Jazz is an important American art form. It is music that was born in the African-American communities of New Orleans.

With the help of some musician friends, Walker formed Jazz House Kids. She taught jazz music classes in local schools in Newark. The classes were fun. Kids loved them. Word spread quickly. Soon Walker was offering more than 15 classes each week.

Today the faculty is made up of over 40 professional jazz artists. They run camps and teach music programs

Melissa Walker performs.

A Jazz House Kids ensemble in 2018.

for at-risk youth. Other programs include a jazz choir and instrumental lessons for students with special needs. In 2013, Walker opened a Jazz House music studio in Montclair. It serves students from nearly 40 communities in New Jersey.

One of Jazz House Kids' biggest programs is the annual Montclair Jazz Festival. It started out as a small event at the end of summer camp. Today more than 10,000 people attend. The festival lasts for two weeks, with over 20 concerts. More than 250 jazz musicians perform.

Many students in the program have won scholarships to major music schools such as Oberlin and Juilliard. Today Jazz House Kids is one of the most respected jazz education programs in the country. Walker now understands that this was her calling.

50,000

Number of young people served by Jazz House Kids

- Melissa Walker started the program in 2002.
- She saw it as a way to give back to students who didn't have access to jazz.
- Over the years, the organization and its students have won over 100 awards.

Ways You Can Help

- Stay in school and always try to do your best work. Get help with subjects you might be struggling with.

- Help others. If you are good at a certain subject, try to help someone who is struggling. Volunteer to tutor or mentor younger students.

- Identify needs in your own school. Then do something to help. For example, you might organize a fundraiser to help buy new library books.

- With help from parents and administrators, organize an after-school enrichment program. It could be an art or chess club, a poetry group, or a fun sport.
- Raise money to donate to an organization that helps in education. Hold a bake sale or a talent show.
- If your school is throwing out textbooks or furniture, find out where you might be able to donate these items.
- With help from parents and administrators, organize a book fair at your school. Collect gently used books and let students take them home for free. Serve refreshments and make it a fun affair.

Glossary

curriculum
Courses taught by a school or college.

dispense
To give or provide something, either for sale or free.

foster
To provide the care that a parent usually gives to a child.

foundation
An organization that uses donated money to help society

GED
A test given to an adult who did not graduate from high school. An adult who passes the test gets an official GED document.

illiterate
Not knowing how to read or write.

inclusive
Open to everyone, not just certain people.

instrumental
Performed on musical instruments.

mentors
People who give help and advice to others who have less experience.

translation
Changing words from one language into another.

trendsetters
People who start a new style or program and make it popular.

volunteer
A person who works without pay in order to help.

Read More

Chopra, Mallika. *Just Breathe: Meditation, Mindfulness, Movement, and More.* Philadelphia, PA: RP Kids, 2018.

Mattern, Joanne. *Barbara Bush.* Edina, MN: Abdo Publishing, 2008.

Norwich, Grace. *I Am: Lebron James.* New York: Scholastic, 2014.

Stewart, Whitney. *Mindful Me: Mindfulness and Meditation for Kids.* Chicago, IL: Albert Whitman, 2018.

Index

About the Author

Patricia Hutchison is a former teacher. She has written dozens of nonfiction children's books about science, nature, history, and geography. She lives in South Carolina with her husband. They love to travel throughout the United States and to other countries.